THE NEW YEARS

Rescue Press, Iowa City
Copyright © 2014 Hannah Brooks-Motl
All rights reserved
Printed in the United States of America
First Edition
ISBN: 978-0-9885873-5-9

Design by Sevy Perez
Cover illustration by Emily Hunt
Text set in Neutraface, Knockout, and FF Tisa
rescuepress.co

THE NEW YEARS

poems by Hannah Brooks-Motl

Mark: Throw a party.
Invite everyone.
My gift will be the biggest.
It says:
Thank You For Being A Friend.

Truly- All my love-

H. E. R. Motl

6/20/14

For my parents

"Fatally, all ideas come from somewhere."

—Jean Rhys

Winter Then

11:00 pm

Bunny
Porch
Girl
Snow

A series a side
Alley to time

*

Ezra Pound was very cold, very white, very much like today, so I spent some hours reading him aloud to my living room. *Not a spare disc of sunlight*. There was a waiting silence I also invented. *This wind is wind of the palace*. Thick, his words fled from me and the snow drained down. *And she went toward the window and cast her down*. Buried in a long dream of hiddenness, the sweep of hair across one's eyes. The *firm even fingers held to the firm pale stone*. Luckily I had bought groceries the night before though in truth I eat very little

Coverlet of snow, its eiderdown
The embarrassment once of not knowing what "counterpane"
meant
A word a lover used in an email
I wrote back a description of the hotel where I was

Also winter then

*

What immovable angles the world has presented this day!
              The boot accumulating its small, insensible horn
          Now, thank goodness, comes afternoon
Burning up morning's melancholic letter

              It is very stark today
                  The white a white
                      Of admonishment

*

Silver in the drear way, the dawn way,
a foal
In flagrant vest some wandered
Oh I went out—

And if I remember other winters
And if other winters mind me
And if it is into reverie I have gone
And if Ezra Pound does not affect me
And if I did not respond
And if it has just been airports and long pulls of time
And if I have been so unwise
And if it has snowed some more upon waking
And if I do not respond
And if reason is gruesome, if the visit is
And if belief neither shrinks
And if I must go on thinking
And if I drive to town despite the weather
And if my arrivals have been ill-advised
And if blankness is a tier
And if I have accumulated, and too uselessly
And if I never respond
And if I sat on my porch in summer also
And if the Bible does not affect me
And if I have shopped
And if I was poor
And if I do not linger much for long
And if I do not write it down
And if this has not been appropriately haphazard
And if this is my only response
And if clarity fights grace
And if this yields experiment
And if I drive to town because of it
And if the road I take depended

To escape is display

To concede knowledge

White roads pour brightest in glare

This is personal somehow

In a tunnel of travel

The ambition of danger

Or swerve through a snare:

I have swerved

And daunted by compass

If I rode on the backs of men

Would I not be king?

The knuckle is tightened

To have slid

Is the frequent conclusion

From the tilt of the sun, something is crumbling

Not burning

Not here

She runs out into it, down the street of it. Her look brushes it from cobblestones, sweeping a path for night's nothing to follow.

She desires it so much she braids her long hair to thousands of braids, framing the scene with want. It continues, and she adjusts.

Walking down the everywhere, into halcyon and lamplight, shedding fat feathers from her coat, she springs a great handful to sky to watch how it's salted. A squirrel blending.

There is little to picture. In trams she is extinguished. Her eyes now mop a slow pool of panic, and graying. She could wander, deciding only.

Very early in morning the buildings persist beneath it. It brings its own mood and is clingy, like her vision scraped through lashes of outrage and detail and use.

When she goes to the bridges it's to avoid thought of the river. Such an elemental turn is engulfing, and everything sticks out of it, in some kind of neutral.

Spires are like stabs in it, all routes are made familiar by it. Once she wrote in her book that she acquiesced, as though belief also were full. The streets heap.

Up into stairwell she tracks it. In bed when she shakes her great hair, the frame alters. Her back no longer a wall, or much value, but she imagines still.

Disregarded, it mucks blackness. She walks alongside this, seeing only her habit of walking, only abutment, requirement, and city. Thus she falls from ornament, into imbue.

All is movement, horrified

Eating my orange hands red

Underground, the love affair leaks out meaning

A woman not unlike the self

Through belittlement and plexiglass

Some fundamental interior—huh, uh-huh

On express

Chase a simple thing

For we plunge just like a lover

Realizing one is afar

In the elaborate country

What is available

What is enough

My lover who would not scratch my head, nor pat

Thinking what may I do

My breathing grown complex

The difficulties of affair being also

An empire

At a moment of danger

The animal acts its thought

With mania of the coterminous

And lost, lost

In the stuffy capsule I have swung my legs

One's inadequacies strewn importantly about

Nothing proper, underground

What of Judgment, Caprice

Affection, Misrule

This little plot I mine

With whom might one argue

Into much scarcity

That distinction is necessary

A common term is

For he would neither graze my cheek nor eye

I have countered

I constructed

Sniffing basic heat on the air

Such is privacy worth gnawing

Among winter garments

In wealth of my birth

Neither budging nor lifting hands

We proceed, underground

Our past misunderstanding

And pure

Goes a man

In gestures of poverty

I have hidden my face

Watching the gap

Swearing dominion, swearing

We too

Endure unprobable tasks

Stand in the stain of the glen
Wave your arms saying all, all of this!

Or go two hillocks high and these
Are your tits

I have a fat will
That leaps, that scents

Drooped on river rock blooming
Under stacks of sky

Some cloudlings with their baldness
Dig a trench

Hearing agony   through the morning's mystery   pride
                    the still river
from which it atrophied   or grew
a lolling castle   picking silver from its teeth
                    and extraordinary
the severe vitality of its core   wafting upward
            like slander, they   came from fear
            a heap of rocks   sorrow waiting
            haul of dirt   the center not a keep
            from their veil something ran

                            and went on running

The murder-hole of friendship

Is above us now

Spitting reason onto my rascally face, you

Are above me now

And undressing, I am

A shivery flank

In some sun

The thing and its trouble both beautiful

Rejoinders

Servile marksmen

Canoeing through ice

In Ireland
Diamond text
Or love writing
Its river
Like men frightened
The shouting, and comfort
The will
Startles keys
My hand
In its hymn

In the street
Kicking rocks high
There is rain
I take stones
Like a purchase
Here in the core
Insignificance
So Hi
To our soft pink
Aspersions

Little pimple

On one's chin

Just awaiting some voluptuousness—

Flayed and then scrubbed

And then sexed

Until fully alone in the widest sense

Because so banal

And numerous

Out here in the dribble

Where spreads disrepute, the wind

Strutting

Someone's fault

So important to be foreign and wise, the small woman thinks
She is drinking a whole ton of beer right now
Her long hair hanging with dark, her dark
Describing some anxiousness

In view of her, we are all equally small
And redolent of self—also tied
To the scene in which flame leaps to fringe
And is stupid

It is significant to stand, to squat, to self-soothe
The small woman glitters correctively
As when we turn our backs
In effort to notice

A riot of surface

Then mist lifts from two bluish eyes; big horizons; of progress believe the obvious metaphors; invisible in most light; no more than chalky piles; not experiences themselves; or vainly imagine the elaborate prosthetic; to approach; not experiences themselves; try various feints and apertures; of acquaintance; of skill; coming home with its knife; stand in the center; nothing has changed; not the experiences themselves; in the round brain; settle cozily; and discouraging; how switch grass marks this field; some night

I take another handful of party mix, dusting the boldness of soiree with grudge

For envy is a strain of sadness

Do I attain a level of accuracy in sequins and fancy dress?

I speak to the mind's striving, to the body's striving

In our sparkle and possible slur

In the honor of event

I contend with the violence of your lack

And wheel hilariously again

When I accuse it is with two varieties of accusation

Because I describe a dual infringement—raw wound of the glass knocked back

Thus the filigree of quarrel

An imagined proximity to the devastating buffet

When I say you had to be there I will tell you why

It is the desire of recollection stalking my face

Fog in Cleveland, and fog in Toledo, so that the horizon mystifies our ability to generalize it, to say that here, yes, the country ended as I end, little niblet of pink. Industry pops up in the sky, oh what do we say

My mother and I sleep two hours at a Flying J, drive on

What is disappointment like? It is like a smoky field, a riven bit of conversation once. I take down notes and we drive, I smell faintly of smoke, and we drive. Through the marks I make, we might decelerate, and this fundamental to the going

Of landscapes trashed with snow, so tidy and lonesome, a material at once fulfilled and yet promising—to be slung into place, I went with my mother, we drove through the day

And safe like some reason for sadness: reading poetry late into night

Arriving, unmet, at an airport

Yet again I was following the border towns through their raw names, counting the silly segues of house, and drive, of poolside, of lawn; all cities with their worth float up ahead as we conceive of travel, taking on variegations like miracles, it is assumption

Dogs in the airport today

Or is it like gravel on the roadside? Pulling through the rifts, embodied on some bus, or is it failure that I can now name its shape that I dragged? What will happen, take its note

Ho-ho the observer, ho-ho the groom

New Years Eve, in the bookshop: "'tis a sad time o' the year" said the woman in the bookshop, marking me home to the hole I stood over again, forming small signs with my hands. These were of practical value, and the streets too were lit. The sun rose. Trains left. I was drunk

My eyes—very beautiful—when drunk

A small flat, a tepid bath, I wake to morning like a dog wakes in onslaught, perhaps the thing shouldn't be named dream. A journey will stare at the one that it jangles, across the lips of whatever I woke there was abandon inside me and in the Victoria & Albert everything gilded, even the taps

Museum-goers with their hungry eyes!

Airports just a terrible null

I listed, my stuff spent, it was spread out in rumor, like a grand past unhappiness, the halls echoed back their heaving of pity, of awkwardness, into forced tenderness, from relief, within lassitude, stupidity

One might find oneself where one has been before, memory proceeds it like waiting. All love affairs shattering down

As at the moment planes take off like fat women, and other women, waiting in the wings, there is pure lift, and then leaving, to acknowledge or to spit out the failure. It was as a puddle icing the wing, perhaps the hot knowledge

Little streets, wooden doors painted white, one arrives at the grocery store in foreign languages, enters the slit, and with a certain quality or like candor one could walk up and down, thus knocking on doors, feeling the might I have done

Cut my thumb washing a knife

My friend to me: "Hannah you're so detached from your animal self"

The French café at last! A little bar squats to one side, some ugly furnishings, it is purple or mauve, Sunday in fact, note the gold coin around the owner's turtleneck, a tiny glass of white wine, stinging with sun

Tact, discretion, mildness, calm, politesse, oh to never disturb another

The skin on my lips peeling, through the vast specter, this evening, or that evening, taking cathedrals safely in hand, throwing the fields, from apartments, their poppies in vase, a whole light, or adjacency, and I move away as one moves away

Man with harp, man with moustache, man eating sandwich
before the flat

Minutes, glass

A bunch of crumbs, his lap

If we look out to the sky it remains a failed shade of blue that we see
The shape of the previous year like a hump under snow in the yard
There is the crooked tree we have always known

In the opposite way, a man we once knew has fallen behind—
We read that his country has fallen
If he lay in the arc of the snow we might make love once again

We love the new year like an object
Or decide to, filling our hands with the unpleasant snow
To type a thing we must be cold

Properly Speaking

Two faces stamped with absence look out at me
Because they are exquisite and misrepresented, I am happy
Look I am my face
You, a lit edge I tiptoe against

It is the most natural thing we say
The heart like all machines
No aspirations, no goals
I take off my shirt because you asked me

But to make a love much less than all this—I rise
To work like a nun
I eat like a nun
I bend like a nun

When you see my image, you must worship

I am not a movie, I insist

Though tonight

I drink many cups of dorm punch

In the snow of ten years back

A sublime confusion

Beats on sublimely

In my chest

Just as I imagine it

Like too I imagine my friends

In tiny heaps of future self

Soar from me, I said

Walking simply across grass

My existence mere toy

I thought it a minute ago

Every other house leans toward the ramshackle,
Which is a kind of enthrallment I guess
In not quite right angles with the past
And hot paints daubing the porch,
Which extends away from the street
Demurely, yet brokenly
Perhaps too close to the next and this
Also a species of pink—
So much color might feel foreign
Were you me
At last
Among strangers
In the long cascade
Of summering

I drive my Corolla down the high road; silver fields beside it; darkness ahead; oh fire behind; like niceness unfastened; I bend my head; in intricate dawn; the fields brimming; some dark remains; or lit up; perhaps I do it; from my sphere; fantastic and pronged; I sit with my head; bowed; it is how I go through my country; like the road; I have felt warm in my car; unable to turn my music down; rushing words from my mouth; for it is dumb to be right; even as trees grow with darkness; complicit; turning the earth as I have been turned; blame cleans my brow; smoothly the road spills like a lie; through somebody; a girl was; through my face; I roll the windows up; down; and when I take a curve; I take it away; into my mind; I open my mouth; thinking I'll speak; dim houses stream faster; like painting; a puddle of chilled water; I put my hand in; the new year is thick; like everyone else; am I incredible; or inside of it

A million fires in my throat, it's funny to laugh—

Not an elegant scorching, no

Because all warmth does welcome, let me take you in

Continuing alone this little bit

For in truth we all wish some more selfish things

A happy gadget with too many parts

Draw the cruel animal closer

Pass out on the couch, ever after believing

We rose early

Say you say you lived here once and I believed this
Thinking bars aren't home, nor travel
When he kissed me I was denatured

We sit in the truck and are not bad
As little kids playing dirty in some snow
Their road the small part of a bigger

What we own is ours like weakness in the coffee or pride
Is everything I can explain away about myself like
What's killing is the weather color

No milk in this river

I apologize for my fatness

I rarely go to the mall for I fear the imperceptible wane of my fear of the mall

One summer I worked in the mall

By then I was so flimsy as to render my fear useless

Though exemplary and there were corridors to it and I hung those with tapestries

Time was a propensity but did not yet exist or not in any case the way I did

Why fear the one road that circles the mall the one circuit it revolves around

In the distance linger some fields and these our grandparents have worked upon

The past drops prettily and in the night of it I feel something at once singular and lush

To be of the multitude is this also lush

The beasts in the fields arrange themselves in a freeing way and it is not unlike the mall

Where a million of us once leaned coolly dangling the idea of a
cell phone

Idea of the spirit likewise hazardous

Step onto this buffed tile for there could be something settled
deep in its black stare

The fountain's shine simply pushed around until I step clear

We have all of us been out striding the crushed stars and called it
the mall

Drink of dollars—I was a person
Back then, I fought
The function of my leisure

Waving the remains of extravagance
I left in a notional sense
For who among us deserves to be rich?

I chronicle an economy of reproof
Reproof I draw like the sea
Uncomfortably yet

In Goodwill polyester
Striding out into evening
My electric friends

A girl's love is different from that of a man, but it cannot be different

A woman in love with a man
The man is beneath her

A woman loving a man who's beneath her

Or lacing the question of dress, or walking out a lot in gardens
Overhead a gruesome metaphysic might rule

Christening the beloved's aspect: "My dear wild boar," this flows

A woman ventures boldly on excursion
Advances slowly after trinkets

Looks out at things with a contemporary look

Never parties for this is before partying, yet offers revelation
In one highly emotional phrase

It is cosmic how much this all matters

Under the hawthorn
The beloved opens his wide tusks and devours a boot

"Love is the greatest labor of women," someone chokes

When my mother dies she will leave me all of her silver
And much of her gold

Come to the table
I jabbered

Speech will often arise
Perceptible, orotund, hesitant, incredible
How much people talk

But I have talked

Everywhere in the world there are lovers in bed
Saying nothing

I won't be prescriptive

Properly speaking, there is power in telling
And saying is cozy, a tête-à-tête
With me on one couch
Recumbent

And tea and beer and mochas:
My family has nothing to say
That I can hear
Any longer

I knew a man
Of great tact

*

A man may be so discreet it is impossible
To find him in public

Circumspection, wariness, wisdom—these are crowns
Of his power
Join him in his huge balloon
Of silence

Discreet
As a courtier
Or one leaf
Falling

Keep an eye on the window, his mouth

*

Saying nothing leads to nothing. This is the truth
About power

The conveyance of talk is not the soul of it

It is soulless
Like gossip

To be found is the least secret of wishes and yet one wishes
These are old affections, the world
I will stay up very late tonight with just this thought

Some bash the world with their popular forms of reckless
They have a solitude of mere convenience
Its door is always open

I ought to go upright and vital. I ought to be less
Splendid. One could while many hours away with watching
These old music videos

Village & Sea

Best friends is meaningless   Lovers also

Wind brings this feeling   Of danger and

Keeping still   At my neck

*

Agreeably announcing "human life is made up of two elements, power and form"

Makes one ridiculous, but then further admit

"It is a flux of moods," which is OK by me

Power is a mood

The small room is, and I stand there on squares

Of setting light

In the morning neighborhood squirrels

Dance like girls

Around some absence

*

I'm just sitting here writing maybe also watching the trees

This tiny view has its hundreds of spines

So repose and be cherished it might urge

I lie down in my kind

*

Take the roof off such moments

Find the intellect

Baffled by a "vast-flowing vigor" flooding

The basement tonight

"We believe in ourselves as we do not believe in others"

Of course I pretend my exceptions

Tracking your path through this clutter

And design

In the sun is where he sits

On the bank still further upon leaves

She lies down among memory like sin

So the dangers of their indulgence

Along streams he tends pridefully his contemplation

Sleeps in melancholy a kind of redemption

Still further than sin she lies down in sin

Rushing along with memory & leaves

Like indulgence among streams

Like he tends sun with danger

Pridefully on the bank she sits

In contemplation further than streams

He sins with melancholy

In memory a kind of sleep

Down in leaves she tends & he sins

Everything along in the down of him

Pridefully they remember leaving

Sitting still in the stream

Danger further along

Covered in memory & too sin

Indulged on the bank in the sun

Then calculate the opened backseat

                                  its stuffing knifed in a smile

                not ours, those guts

                       spilled oilless

       insurrectionary, careening

                    they were not

our guts   but quondam carburetor, piston;

          both headlights

                  plucked

*

Even when I fought   which I did not, the rug woven slightly,

        spare

          tassel of twigs & the spinney's pattern

it was my own skin

         on the birch peeling cleanly as though letting

             a sun burn burn

is an answer

     stupid answer

*

Tree-of-heaven, salicaire

                  wild parsnip, grape: Creeping Charlie
      spanned our view   caitiff weed with riot in his belly
              made of thicket

some mossy dress

              louche willow leaves torn like torn dollars

on my tits

                *

Noise provokes noise, I see it   abandoned in men
              their holler & stretch
  on unfit beds fit for prosper, & scent
               is handful of what, but this
is home, this is home you whisper   in the zenith
      and I heard

What is more retro than train sound than baritone wind, obscure
As movements of neighbors

They catch you at goofing

Because girls also being wind here and mouth here take this little reed
You seemingly forgot and practice

Into morning, become marching
Onto track fields, desire spending

This is some beautiful cash, some beautiful inkling

You live like a globe in the town. Let fly
Prognostications:

You will be lit forever with sweetness
You disperse the meaning

It is not boring being so boring, it is flouncy

One must wear ripped-up jeans and glide
Through the fixed mouth of morning
Road signs may startle to one's left and one's right like deer
Or importunate memory
It will be both very late and early
The self too will dawn, nicely hideous—one should hide from it
For everything today will be inadequate
Slackly the fine thigh enters the car
And exits
All things swim in this glitter

Boyfriends emit some kind of light and yet discussion was not love. *I woke up among the morning's slab of marble, sea, or ice.* Or I woke up in minutes, bucketing down. I collected them and attempted bad soliloquy. Above me grew a vacancy of great though accidental beauty—was it skylight or some knots in wood? *I also had no real wishes at this point.* I touched my thighs again.

Struck with longing. The parked car. *Forced from failure.* My neighbor trundling. I watch him trundle. *I long and park my car.* Seen from the second floor here, I am hair. From the ground—a pair of blades. We cannot keep to the serious business of being village *and have no wish to.* My neighbor trundles. His wife swipes at her snowed-in car. From my window I have removed my curtain, my shirt, the sound of my voice coming. *The various delights to also fail in.*

Bedroom skylight
Bedroom window

For the paint was not immodestly chosen, nor applied. Out of wilderness of course comes some invention. As I have seen those babies walking. *I pretend to like a lot of things, and know things too.* Out of wilderness must come a fence, mind to lock the trashy heirloom in.

Each backyard holds out its palm. And the fist: to be balled and swung or worked or hit upon. *These too are deceiving labors of the meek.* I tread carefully down the stub of stairs, filling space with glory. It was not lawn they sought *and yet geometry was applicable, and applied.* I made such calculations in another life and covered them with tone. *For shame the distance and for shame the backs of men.*

I have two windows in this room—a square of white, a square of blue. Art my grandma made: an eagle at rest on a branch. *It is 1975.* And I will never be alive. *Granny Speer,* Granny Speer. *What a spot of ruin here.* And the desk I ache.

Living Room
Kitchen

Some run this short wide corridor. As I go work lush silence. And cut my fingertips, this too I do in the kitchen. *Waiting for bread.* Which is the finest thing—that we remember men or believe in them. Here at the sink. *It was done at the sink.* This was the secret to life. Moving around a lot. I listened and listened some more. *To the mix.*

Solder and some dullish glass. *Because block me in.* A bevelled thing, pitched in ponds. *And all around me struck belovedness.* I will not stare out or in so much. But take my apple and toast my bread. *Because I live all day.* When she pieced this one together she had never even seen a mountain.

Front porch

Out beyond the little family, I wish it made of dusk.

Garage, lace curtain, the scallop

Of a door

Exceptional natures bear my neighbors

One cloaked shadow in their backyard

Exactly the shape of a too-nice car

I meander near the edge

Of discourse with the other in the self

Hey there say the trees across my house's head

Though not to other trees I guess

I nap under the pine's furry banner. Your mother's voice is the sound of
        birds around me—
She is telling a story about being poor

Fields seethe extravagant green air—I pet a dog who died last year. How
        delectable I was then
Along the telescopic shore

The houses are so pompous here on this corner, someone whispers
        through wind I keep ambling—
Daffodils grow in patches of immeasurable distance, but O
            To be smoking
                With prim obscurity
                    On the pied scoops of mountains

When I go for my run it is art that I do—into the prairie!

There may be a yellow barn on the route—let us name it transcendence

I hear the sound of earth coming up through the leaves—all upon the prairie!

The mind runs along, full of misconduct—inescapable desire for censure

He thought she was hot he told me and he liked her tattoos—unexpected desire for censure!

There are clouds that pursue, and pursue, and pursue—high above the surfeit of prairie

Striving to memorize the initial flash of reminding—pain is very accurate!

She laughed but did not laugh she wrote me—I too used to eat less

What good to speak now to love's endlessness—like litter over the prairie

Grass may hide devastations from view—how extensive the look of the prairie!

My voice continues inside me, both small and yet serious—it embodies an incident

I have learned to ignore it—

It was a small hotel

On the sea

All arrayed

Against the huger sky

Every time

A new guest came

We could think about

The small hotel

Each new guest made

The nothing out the window

On the street

Hooked around us

In gusts

Ocean curled

Its great torn arm

Obliging seals

Dunes were bullied

In a brain

One was like

A pearlish gull

Thinking only

Of how it was

Just the essence

Like convention

In fragrant houses

And through these lanes

Or now I think

There are distracted climes

Like these

People wall

Their gardens in

Wall

Their own distraction

And behind it

Bloom strange blooms

And alabaster

A small dog, woofing

In flights of rain

The past comes

Rushing to its place

And this is certain

False, and God

A timid ruin

Takes collection

How like knowing

What was willful

In this a cliff

Seemed forming

I climbed it on my bike

And riding out

A thin coat flapped

Through the fields

Of drinking and the joke

To rattle slowly

On at home

Then out to work

And past the beach

One had some purpose

By the sink

Becoming proficient

At this station

Laying knives

Light fixtures swung

Nasty and cheap

It was a fast urge

The delight

I stood

In a darkened hall

More darkened hall

To what have small hotels

Been witness?

Proprietors, appropriate

And dim

Tartan carpet

A bunch of gorse

The manageress undressing

In the kitchen

Just some chef

Who ogled

Perhaps in trust of life

Its simple shapes

The inner wrong

I deserved

The things he called

Sheets and pebbles

Violet light

Took a pen shell like a pen

And wrote this down

A strong wealth

Came over me

Folding napkins

I could not share it

It cast me out

Comprehension, be distinct

Where we wander

And what follows

From maps of cloud

With happy sharpness

On a happy ledge

*

When I think of you it is spring, and very real
You walk, springing up
Count on your two hands beating
Coming through—you are spring, making way
Along the green, pebbled path and the generated
Soul wells up, like some water
Must I drink

Ahead of me, there are ghosts
Do I know them
Their names, particular looks, and a certain
Singing nature

It's possible I have spoken
Nonsense, and before you
The night pushes in past stone walls,
Swept yard, the new house
And window

Ahead of me, there are ghosts
Do I need them
Their real knowledge or my own
Faceless showing

The head is your spring and being walked
Through the hills, a black field—
Where is your soft, suburban grotto
To go to, again
Is it handsome

Notes

Many of these poems record, respond, and react to reading. And so many of them owe significant debts of language or inspiration to other writers—"the ones I like who are dead," in the words of W.S. Graham. These include: Roland Barthes, Isaiah Berlin, John Cage, Ralph Waldo Emerson (especially), Richard Hugo, Michel de Montaigne, Ezra Pound, Henry David Thoreau, and W.B. Yeats.

This book also exists because of many small and large acts of friendship and faith. Many thanks to Dan Bevacqua, Stephen Burt, Francesca Chabrier, Michele Christle, the Daroms, Douglas Dunn, Ben Estes, Peter Gizzi, Elizabeth Haas, Emily Hunt, Daniel Khalastchi, Mark Leidner, Mollye Miller, Kieran Mulhall, the Nissenboim-Rices, JoAnna Novak, Caryl Pagel, Vicky Paine, Alice Pedersen, Don Paterson, John Redmond, Nick Rose, Zach Savich, Stacy Jo Scott, Caitlin Spies, Allison Stephenson, James Tate, C.S. Ward, Betsy Wheeler, Caitlin Wick, Dara Wier, and (especially) all the Brooks-Motls.

Versions of some of these poems first appeared in *District, Everyday Genius, jubilat, Petri Press, Sixth Finch,* and the anthology *This Land.* Thanks to the editors of these journals.

Hannah Brooks-Motl was born and raised in Wisconsin. A chapbook, *The Montaigne Result*, was published by The Song Cave in 2013. She holds an MFA from the University of Massachusetts-Amherst and currently lives in Chicago, where she is a PhD student at the University of Chicago. *The New Years* is her first book.

RESCUE PRESS